The Little Civil

By Jemma Quin

Copyright 2022 by Jemma Quin

All rights reserved.

No part of this book may be reproduced or stored in a retrieval system or transmitted in any form or by any means, electronic, mechanical, photocopying, recording, or otherwise, without the express written permission of the author Jemma Quin.

Thank you for reading this book. You have made this engineer very happy.
My first book "The Adventures of a Little Engineer" is also available on Amazon.
I am also a STEM Ambassador who visits schools showing children the wonderful world of Science, Technology, Engineering, and Maths.
If you would like a bulk order or to arrange an author visit to your school feel free to get in touch via LinkedIn and we can arrange that.

Please note this book has been self-published and edited, so there may still be spelling and grammar mistakes. Please be kind to the author and feel free to tell your child the correct spelling.

LinkedIn

To my family and friends.

Thanks for supporting me on my mad adventures.

Here are two little storied about Jemma's Adventures in Engineering called:

The Little Civil Engineer and the Crane

And

The Little Civil Engineer Who Found Her Calling

Now before we begin there this one thing to do. The little Civil Engineer, needs a name:

The little Civil Engineer is called:

……………………………………………………………………..

When it says The Little Civil Engineer,

use this name instead.

The Little Civil Engineer And The Crane

She went to site to help her friends.
To lift a heavy load.
They planned to use a little crane.
Which fit nicely on the road.

She got to site and had a look.
To check what had arrived.
And found they'd sent a bigger crane.
Which could not get inside.

So, she had a look at the route to site.
To see if there was another way.
For the crane to reach the other gate.
Which seemed miles away.

Help the Little Civil Engineer get to site:

"Ah ha!" she said suddenly.
When she found the answer.
She quickly drew a detailed map.
And handed it to the driver.

When the crane arrived,
she did her checks,
and looked it up and down.
But the mats they had were for
a little crane.
To sit upon the ground.

So, she did some sums to check the mats.
To see if they would do.
But the mats were not big enough!
Whatever would they do?

MATT, $L = 1m$, $B = 1m$

$$\text{AREA} = L \times B = 1 \times 1 = 1 m^2$$

SLEEPERS, MATT, 2m × 2m

$$\text{AREA} = L \times B = 2 \times 2 = 4 m^2$$

$$\text{FORCE} = \perp \text{ OUTRIGGER LOAD} = 800 kN$$

$$\text{GROUND BEARING PRESSURE} = \frac{\text{FORCE}}{\text{AREA}}$$

just MATT $= \frac{F}{A} = \frac{800}{1} = 800 kN/m^2$

MATT + SLEEPERS $= \frac{F}{A} = \frac{800}{4} = 200 kN/m^2$

ALLOWABLE GROUND BEARING $P = 300 kN/m^2$

$200 kN/m^2 < 300 kN/m^2$ ∴ ok

"We need to get some bigger mats!"
So, she jumped back in her van.
And went along to the stores, because she had a plan.

In the stores she found some sleepers.
Which are big bits of wood.
If she stacked them underneath the mats,
then work together, they would.

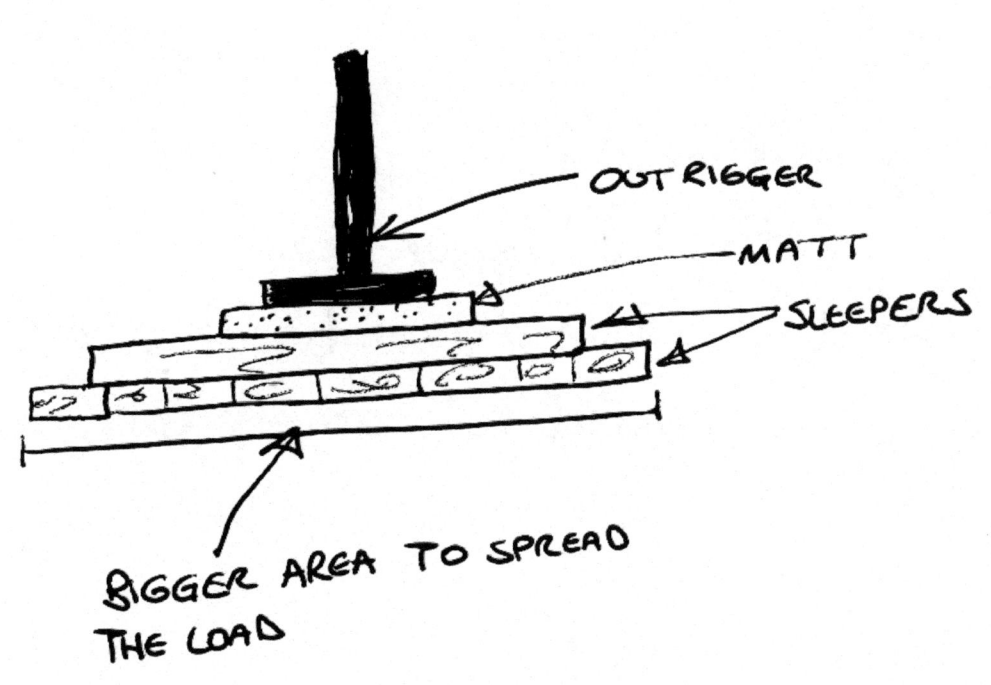

This would be equivalent,
to the bigger mats.
And save the driver having to
go back and get some parts.

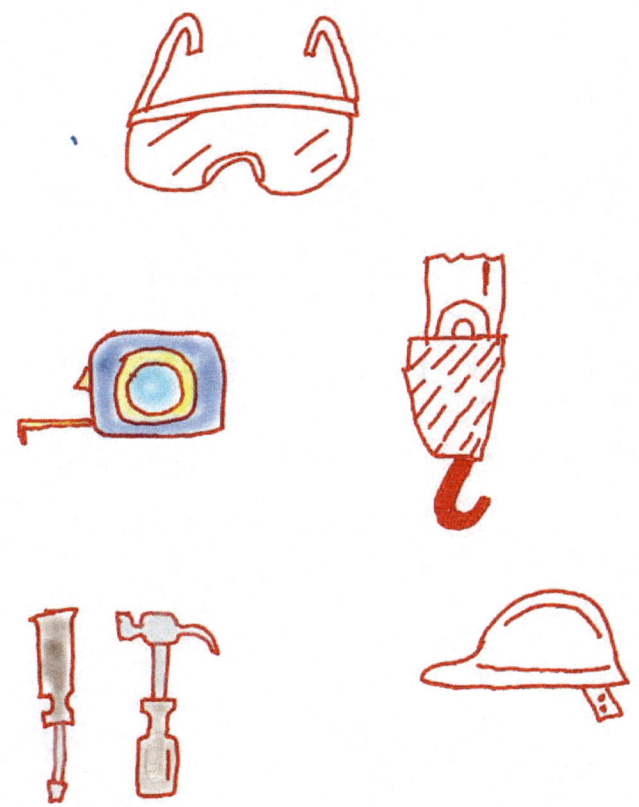

She double checked her maths,
and got her friend to check.
That her plan all made sense
and her sums were correct.

So finally, they set up the crane, and did their safety checks. Everything was set up right, and they could lift things up in nets.

But an engineer's job is never done,
and soon she found another problem.
So, she packed her tools and headed off.
Her lunch break was forgotten.

She loved her job on days like this.

When she was super busy.

And got to solve lots of problems.

Even when things got in a tizzy.

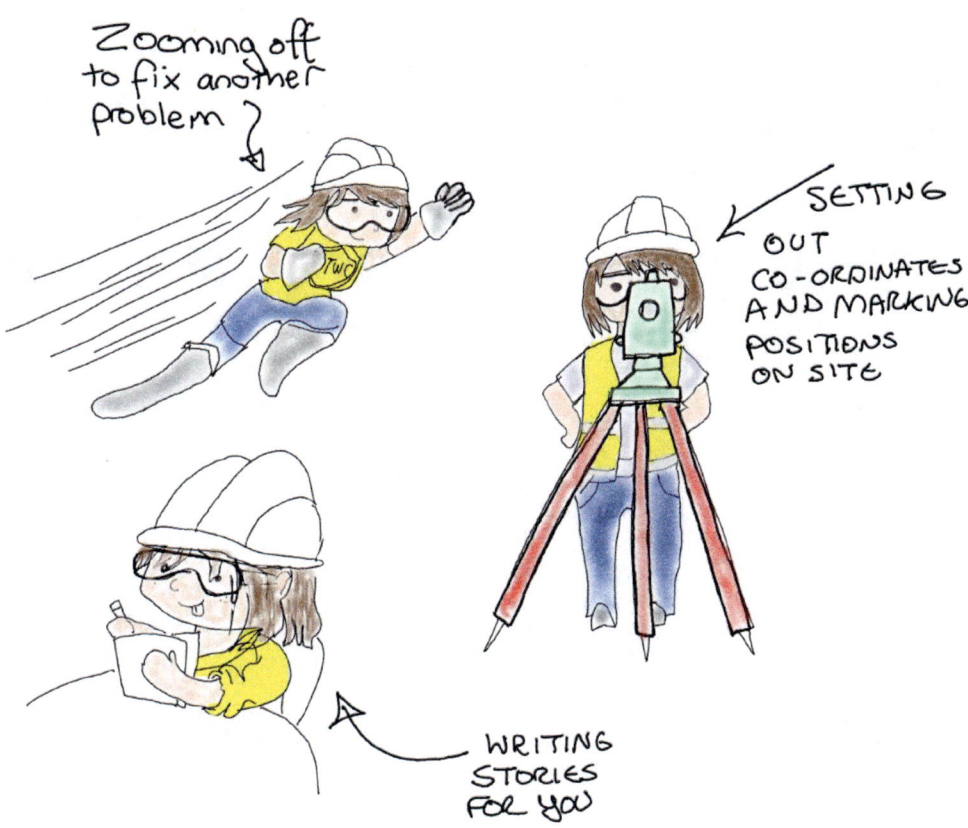

The Little Civil Engineer Who Found Her Calling

To help her get chartered she learned how to design, lots of complex engineering which took a long, long time.

Help the little engineer design this by joining the dots together. Start at number 1. Can you guess what it is?

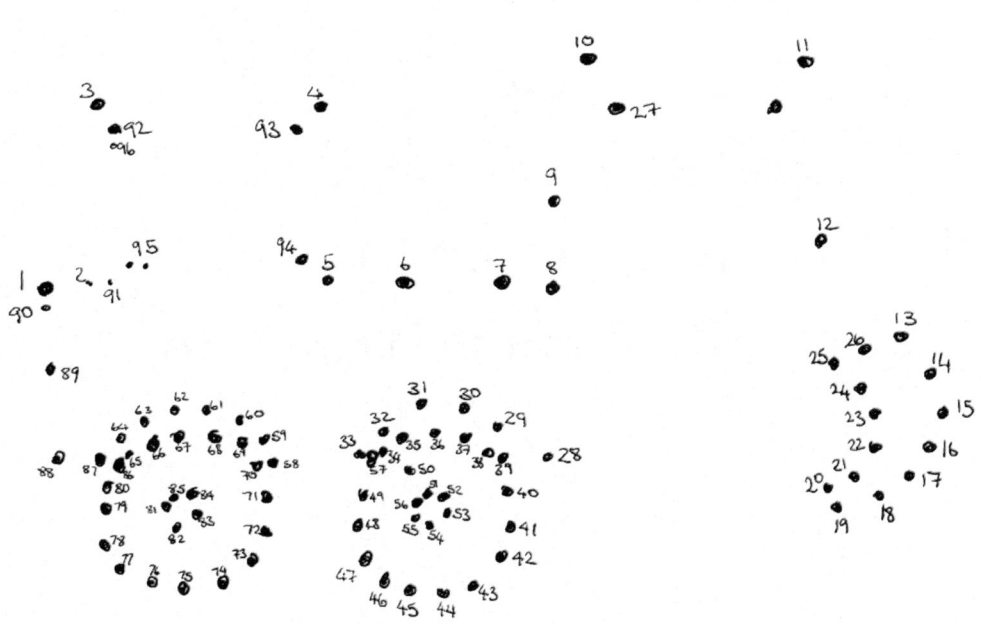

At first, she was a little scared,
that she couldn't do it.
But with some encouragement
she sailed right through it.

Colour in the picture:

Once she understood the basics.
Like what is a force?
It's something that pushes or pulls.
Like a cart pulled by a horse.

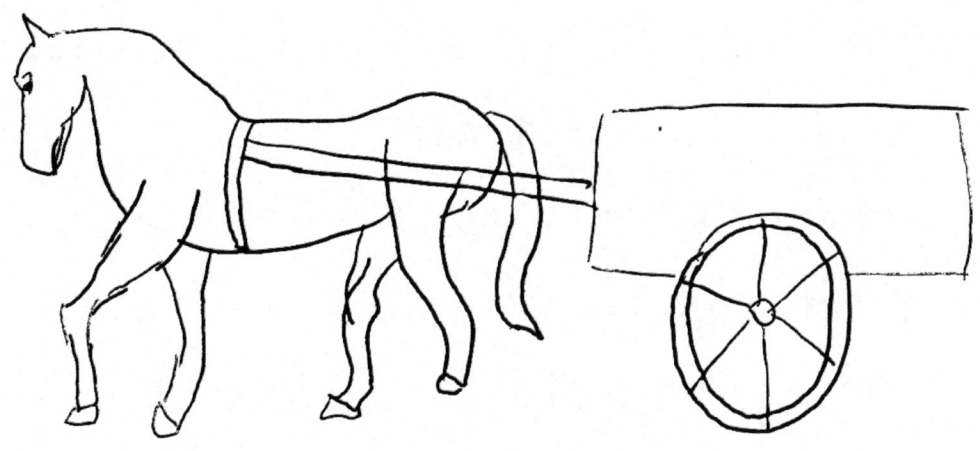

A "moment" is not just a point in time.
Sometimes called an instance.
It causes things to overturn.
Its force times distance.

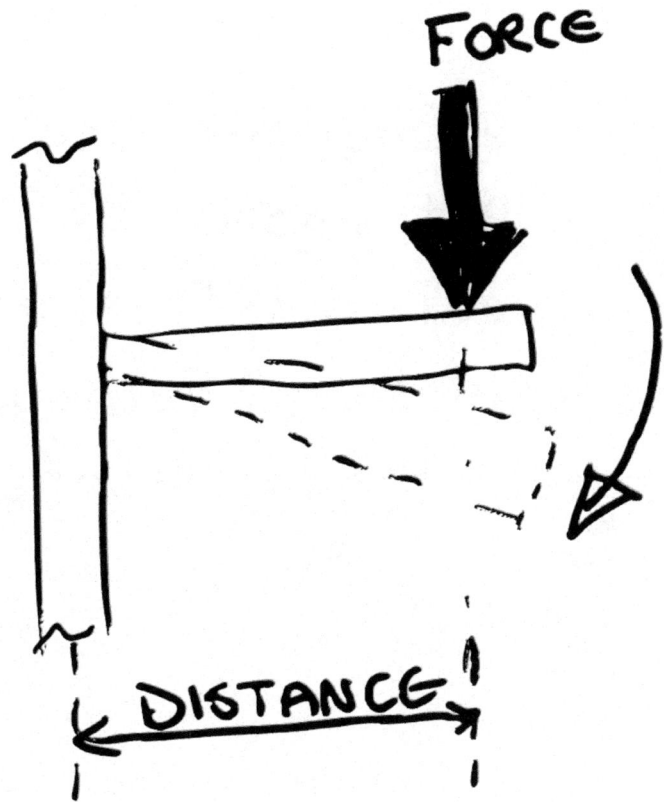

Sometimes she used
Pythagoras,
to work out complex shapes.
Like angles and octagons
or great big landscapes.

Her favourite things to design were concrete shutters.
Because they reminded her of cake tins.
Just like her grandmother's.

Her Gran's recipe for Chocolate Concrete (also known as Rocky Road):

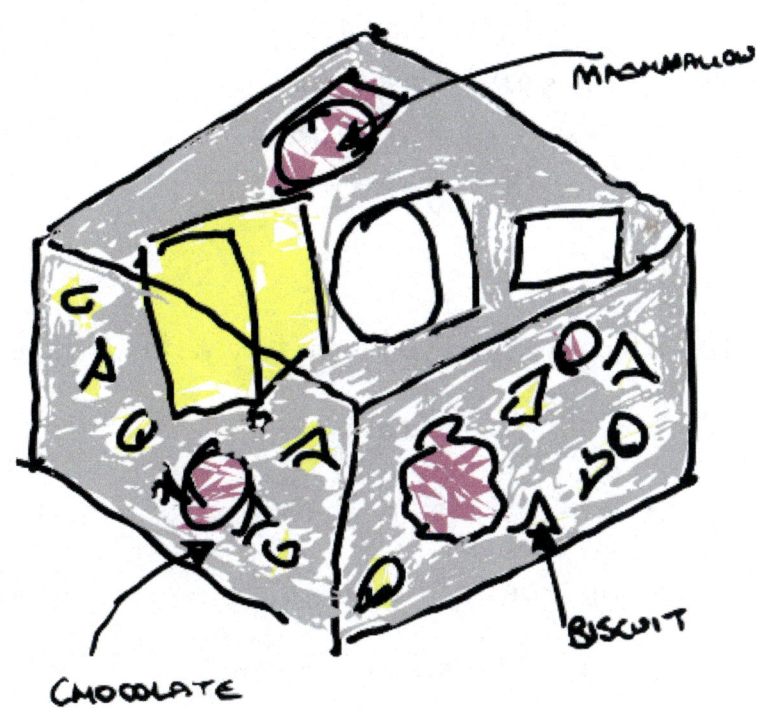

Ingredients:
200g digestive biscuits
135g butter
200g chocolate
2-3 spoons of golden syrup
100g mini marshmallows
Icing sugar to dust

1. Grease and line a baking tin with baking paper.
2. Place the digestives in a bag and break up into small pieces (She likes to use a rolling pin to smash them).

3. Melt the butter, chocolate, and golden syrup over a gentle heat. Stir until it's all melted and remove from the heat.
Allow to cool slightly.
4. Add the biscuits and marshmallows to the chocolate and stir until everything is covered in chocolate.
5. Tip the mixture into the lined baking tin and spread out to the corners. Chill for at least 2 hours and then dust with some icing sugar.
Cut into pieces and enjoy.

You made your shape out of wood,
and poured in wet concrete.
Then waited for it to gain strength,
which sometimes took all week.

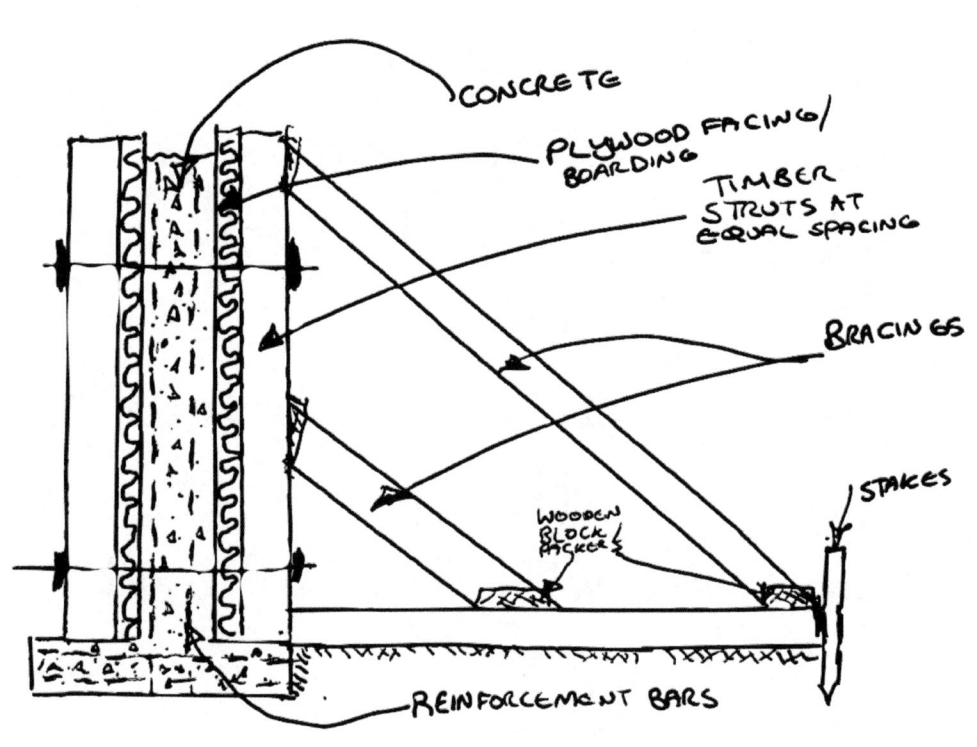

She learned a new type of engineering.
It was called "Temporary Works."
It soon became her favourite thing,
and came with lots of perks.

Can you find all the words?

Engineer,
Crane,
Design,
Bridge,
Force,
Moment,

Site,
Concrete,
Little,
Shutter,
Temporary
Works

T	E	M	P	O	R	A	R	Y	W	O	R	K	S
H	I	M	O	M	E	N	T	H	Y	E	B	Z	S
C	O	N	C	R	E	T	E	S	H	U	T	T	A
S	O	P	S	I	T	E	F	C	H	I	O	E	K
T	R	Q	J	S	H	S	E	C	T	H	B	O	C
O	S	H	U	T	T	E	R	R	S	X	E	I	T
R	Z	L	E	I	N	A	E	A	E	O	U	L	H
Y	G	O	D	N	N	O	O	N	M	B	C	J	O
O	I	V	E	N	G	I	N	E	E	R	I	N	G
R	C	E	S	K	E	T	A	R	D	I	S	W	A
C	I	L	I	T	T	L	E	C	R	D	E	M	S
Q	H	S	G	Y	R	O	L	A	F	G	M	T	Z
B	Y	Z	N	H	Z	F	O	R	C	E	T	E	A
S	U	R	P	R	I	S	E	Z	J	S	U	M	E

57

It's something that supports a structure,
when you build or take it down.
Or supports a piece of plant (like a crane),
that's sitting on the ground.

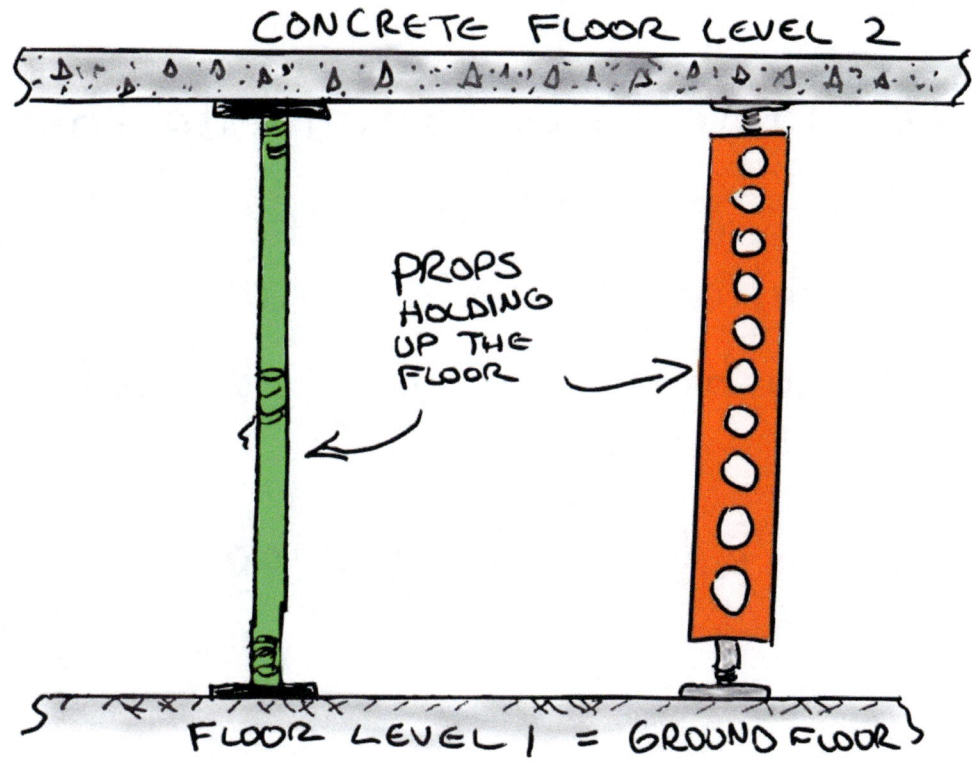

It's something to hold up the earth,
when you dig a hole.
Or to help you reach a high place,
like the top of a pole.

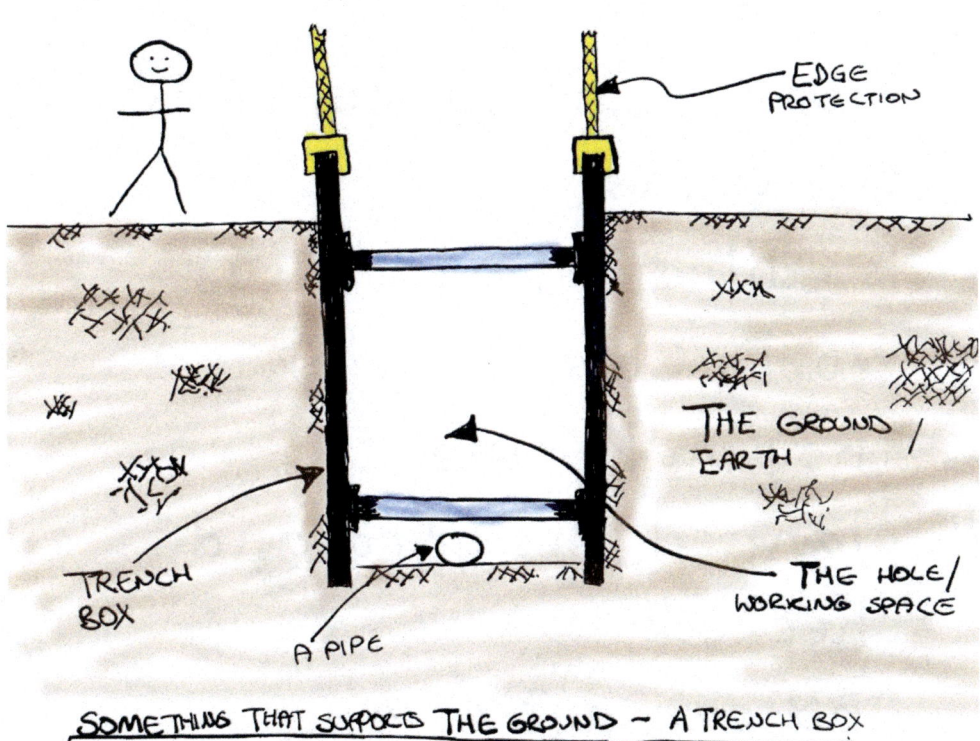

The person who controls the works
is called a Temporary Works Co-ordinator.
They make sure its planned, designed and checked
And can act as a translator.

Morse Code:

A .- / B -... / C -.-. / D -.. / E . /
F ..-. / G --. / H .... / I .. / J .--- /
K -.- / L .-.. / M -- / N -. / O --- /
P .--. / Q --.- / R .-. / S ... / T - /
U ..- / V ...- / W .-- / X -..- /
Y -.-- / Z --.. / , --..-- /
full stop .-.-.-

Help The Little Civil Engineer translate this:

A CIVIL ENGINEER IS SOMEONE WHO BUILDS INFRASTRUCTURE SUCH AS ROADS, BRIDGES, SEWERS AND BUILDINGS.

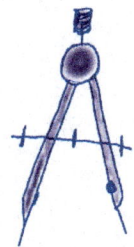

It takes lots of different people,
to get the job done right.
The **TWC** brings them all together.
working day and night.

(The TWC is the Temporary Works Coordinator)

Draw a picture of people working together:

She soon realised.
That's what she'd like to be.
Someone who brings people together.
she'll be a **TWC**.

Here is some useful QR codes if you want to find out more about Jemma and Civil Engineering:

Some info about Jemma

What is Civil Engineering

Here are some pictures for you to colour in

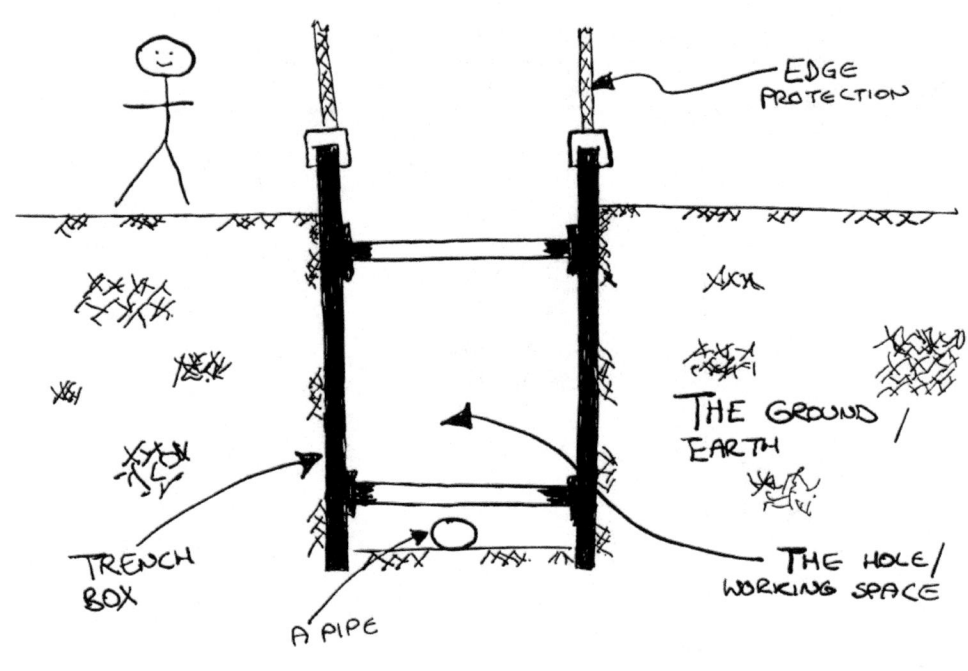

SOMETHING THAT SUPPORTS THE GROUND ~ A TRENCH BOX

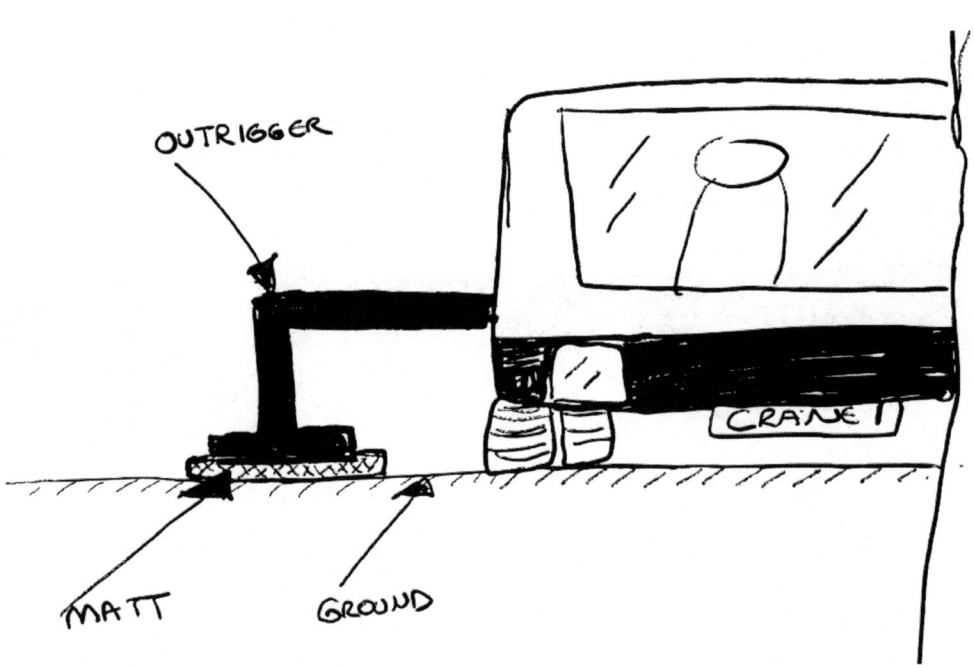

Printed in Dunstable, United Kingdom